MONEY-SMART MILLENNIALS

MONEY-SMART MILLENNIALS
HOW TO BE FINANCIALLY STABLE
IN YOUR TWENTIES AND THIRTIES

LIONEL Y. HOUNKANRIN

Money-Smart Millennials: How to Be Financially Stable in Your Twenties and Early Thirties

For more information, visit www.moneysmartmillennials.com or write to: lionel@moneysmartmillennials.com.

Please share about this book with your friends and family.

To my beautiful wife Heather and
your unwavering support in everything I
attempt to do;
To my parents, Jerome and Melanie who have
instilled in me hard work;
To my brothers, Orphee and Gallus who are an
inspiration every day;
And to all the friends and family who have
played a role in my life;
Thank you.
This book is dedicated to you.

CONTENTS

Introduction

Are you today between the ages of eighteen and thirty-five? If you are, then you are a millennial like me. Or do you consider yourself a millennial? If so, this book was written for you. Do you know family, friends, co-workers and acquaintances who are millennials? Of course, you do. *Money-Smart Millennials* was also written for you so that you acquire the knowledge to educate or simply offer them the opportunity to read the book. Since I am a millennial myself, many times in this book I write in the first person.

Per the US Census Bureau, millennials are 83.1 million strong, more than a quarter of the population and we outnumber the 75.4 million baby boomers[1]. We matter. After working for a couple of years in the financial industry and particularly in banking, I realized that there is a problem: many of us are struggling financially. We have not been educated on financial literacy; we hope to be in a better position a few years from today, but we do not have the resources and the knowledge to get there. This handbook is for us.

I want to congratulate you for deciding to read *Money-Smart Millennials: How To be Financially Stable in Your Twenties and Early Thirties*. First, what does 'money-smart' mean? It is a state of mind in which a person deals wisely with the challenges associated with money management and recognizes and capitalizes on opportunities to expand his or her income. Most likely, you have a financial goal which you are trying to accomplish. You may simply want to understand your finances better and how to manage your money. You may also be very stable financially and want to improve. In either case, you have made the necessary step. Many will only complain about their situation, but never take action. You on the other hand took responsibility and my hat is off to you. You have demonstrated that you want to be in control of your life.

When I was crafting the title *'Money-Smart Millennials: How to Be Financially Stable in Your Twenties and Early Thirties'*, one of my main goals was to convey that this book is not going to be another investment guide. It is not a step-by-step guide to wealth. As I was driving and thinking about a title on my way to work one day, the word street-smart came to mind. Street-smart is an adjective used to describe a person who has a know-how in the affairs of life, a thought process that is not taught through the formal education system. I had an epiphany. 'Money-smart' came to mind and for the next few days, I couldn't think of anything else. It is simple and it describes perfectly the content of the book.

The concepts I bring up are not taught in most schools. 'Money-Smart' became the appropriate word. The purpose of *Money-Smart Millennials* is to teach a mindset. I want to instill in you habits and a thought-process about your money which will lead to financial stability. For me, being financially stable means:

1. Make a large enough income to cover all your expenses and save a substantial amount of it.

2. Build an emergency fund large enough to cover your expenses for six to twelve months if you were to lose your source of income.

3. Have no debt or a very minimal amount of money owed to creditors.

There is no foundation for wealth if there is no financial stability. Many individuals attain sudden wealth only to lose it for lack of the mindset you are about to learn. Did you know that four out of ten people who win the lottery are broke within five years? A third of them files for bankruptcy which indicates that they are in a worse financial position than they were prior to winning the jackpot[2]. By the time you are done reading 'Money-Smart Millennials', you will know how to:

- Create a budget and live by it.

- Manage your bank accounts and your debt.

- Make decisions that lead to financial stability.

- Create additional income to reach your goals.

I hope this book helps you in your journey to becoming a money-smart millennial. It is time to be confident about your finances. It is time to be independent and finally leave mom and dad's nest. At age eighteen, I started a journey thousands of miles away from my parents. Along the way, I received help and mentorship from tremendous people. My road wasn't always easy, but by applying the money-smart mindset, I was able to pay for my college education, pay for a car, live without any debt at times and establish savings. Today, I am married to the most beautiful woman in the world and together, we have achieved financially stability. Now, it is your turn.

Enjoy the book. Share it with other millennials. Visit **moneysmartmillennials.com** and join me by subscribing to get exciting resources and articles. And most importantly, become a MONEY-SMART MILLENNIAL.

Part I

Martin Luther King Jr. Memorial by Lionel Hounkanrin

Chapter I: The reality of the situation

[While] our survey found financial stress rising among all employees for the first time in the past five years, [...] 64 percent of millennials indicated that they were stressed. - Kent E. Allison (The Huffington Post)[1]

Millennials represent more than a quarter of the population of the United States. We have exceeded the baby boomers in numbers. We are the largest generation in the workforce; we are all about startups and we want to take over organizations[2]. There is countless research done on what millennials want, what we value, our living habits, our work habits, our spending habits and many other topics. I am sure that you have come across an online article describing the behavior of millennials in the workplace. It has even become a marketing trend for business and human resource consultants.

Here are a few characteristics of this generation of dreamers[3]:

- We are entrepreneurial and we want more challenging opportunities.

- We are a connected generation and we want a casual, laid back work environment. We like a coach, not a boss.

- We want a healthy work life balance.

I believe the millennial generation will change the world. Our times have yet to discover what young people aged 18 to 35 are capable of accomplishing. The days of geniuses such as Henry Ford and more recent Steve Jobs and Bill Gates are not over. And if you think this generation will not see another Mark Zuckerberg, I strongly believe that you are soon to be marvelously surprised. We are on the verge of a universal transformation and it will come from this generation of millennials. Wait and see.

Success is truly a time bomb and cannot be sustained when one does not know how to manage his or her money.

This all sounds great and inspiring, but what good is it for millennials to succeed but lack financial literacy? I know we all want to create the next Facebook, develop killer apps and software, run impactful nonprofit organizations and travel around the world. However, success is truly a time bomb and cannot be sustained when one does not know how to manage his or her money. Your income, small or incredibly large, does not determine your financial stability. If you speak the language of financial literacy as I speak Russian - not a bit -, your income will find its way out of your hands very fast. But on the contrary, knowing how to be financially stable will determine how far your income goes.

Heather and I live in the Washington D.C. area and specifically in Montgomery County, Maryland. It is one of the richest counties in the country. There is no lack of wealth surrounding us. However, after working just a few months at the bank, it was clear to me that there is an unbelievable number of people who make six figure incomes, but have absolutely nothing to show for it. I once cold a called client who lived in a $500,000 house to sell her a credit card. She drove a Lexus and if I remember correctly, her husband also drove a luxurious car. They had bought on credit every single piece of furniture in the house and were also paying on student loans. She couldn't wait to get this credit card to consolidate other debt. I was so shocked to realize that she had been declined the credit card despite the double six figure income in their household. This is the case of thousands of families I have come in contact with. On the outside, it looks perfect, but on the inside, there is roaring financial chaos. They spend their income to start every month at zero dollars. Do not be fooled by your friends' luxurious cars, their big houses and the beautiful photos of their exotic vacations on Facebook and Instagram.

Unfortunately, too many times it is the cover of a book whose story you will find very depressing. We live in a culture of credit cards and debt. Fellow millennials, I urge you to be aware of the danger.

A few statistics on millennials

- In 2013, 25-year-old millennials had an average balance of $20,926 in student loans[4].

- According to economist Jeremy Rifkin, in 25 years, millennials will be sharing vehicles and not owning them. This trend has already started today and we see more startups which provide rental of products without any ownership commitment. This may be due to the fact that millennials are not yet to afford these products.

- They do not pay their bills on time. One out of four millennials has fallen behind on their dues and has been added to the collection list of creditors[5].

- When it comes to credit scores, this generation has the lowest.

- Unbelievably, seventy percent of this generation expect to live on less than $36,000 after retirement. Fifteen percent think they will win the lottery and another eleven percent are assuming they will be 'gifted' retirement funds[6].

- "Many millennials began their adult lives in the midst of the worst economic downturn in generations, and our survey reveals just how deeply and broadly the Great Recession has marked the financial lives of this generation of Americans. Unfortunately, far too many millennials trying to cope with these economic conditions have low levels of financial literacy and are wrestling with concerns about their debt," - FINRA Foundation President Gerri Walsh[7].

We live in times that require change and action. If you are from an older generation and you've decided to read this book, I want to thank you for it. I will need your help in educating my fellow millennials because you are more likely to be in a better financial situation. Nonetheless, I believe that you will benefit as well from the principles I mention in *Money-Smart Millennials*.

On the other side, you may be a millennial reading this book and not relating at all. You are very knowledgeable with proper money management and your finances are in great shape. I applaud you because that's the goal. *Money-Smart Millennials* will confirm and enhance your financial literacy.

However, for the majority of millennials the outlook on finances is not pleasant. It is in fact very alarming. As a millennial, I am very anxious about our future. If nothing is done, I am afraid of what the finances of millennials twenty years down the road will possibly look like. With a ton of debt, bad credit scores, insufficient incomes, no savings, inexistent retirement plans and the ignorance of financial principles, there is no hope. So, let's start this journey together. It is not a long one; it may be difficult at times, but it sure is a simple one. I can't wait to share with you the principles that I have applied in my life which have led me today to a financial position I am proud of.

Chapter II: It all starts with a definite financial goal and a deadline to achieve it

Our goals can only be reached through a vehicle of plan, in which we must fervently believe and upon which we must vigorously act. There is no other route to success. - Pablo Picasso

In high school, your goal was to graduate. When you enrolled in college, you knew you had to graduate a certain number of years down the road, depending on the degree you were pursuing. When your eyes caught the beautiful blonde walking down the hall, your mind was consumed by one thought. You had a goal: to get her number. I can guarantee you that ninety percent of the time, the first question a personal trainer would ask you prior to working with you will be regarding the fitness goal you are trying to accomplish. We set objectives in practically every compartment of our lives. Therefore, my question to fellow millennials is this: why do you only 'wish' that you were in a better position financially? Why do you only

What are we doing today to change our circumstances? The answer to that question determines where we will be in a few years.

hope to have more money in your savings account? Why do you only dream of being out of debt? Why haven't you chosen the destination? Wishes, dreams, feelings and tears do not add $5,000 to your checking account. Whether it is adding $10,000 to your savings account by the end of the year, reducing your debt by $3000 or making an additional $500 per month, it is important to pinpoint that spot on the map where you would like to end up. Here is the most important question that we, as millennials, should ask ourselves: what are we doing today to change our circumstances? The answer to that question determines where we will be in a few years. If you do not have a specific response, it is time to take control.

Step I: Choosing your goal

Have you ever watched a soccer match? Every time a team scores it is an outburst of emotions preceded by the commentator yelling GOOOOOALLLLLL!!!! If you don't believe me, search 'Top 15 Crazy Commentators of all time' on YouTube. Financial goals are the object of our effort and when they are reached, they deserve the same enthusiasm and excitement.

Here are a few examples of financial goals that millennials came up with:

- I will have $5,000 saved.

- Next year, I will need a new car. I will finance no more than $20,000 and I will have at least $4,000 saved as a down payment.

- In a few years, my wife and I will start shopping for a new house. Our goal is to have $50,000 saved as a down payment.

- I have $15,000 in student loan debt. My goal is to pay it off in just a few years.

- We currently have four credit cards. We will pay off three so that we only have one with a balance.

- I have been saving about $400 every month and I will double that amount very soon.

It is great. You have come up with a goal. Notice that in the examples, they used 'will' in place of 'want', 'hope' and 'wish'. 'Will' brings in the commitment aspect. To succeed, we must be serious and willing to be dedicated. Simply wishing for an objective opens the door for excuses and for procrastination.

After doing this exercise of writing goals

with a few millennials, many of them showed excitement, but expressed that something was missing. Though the financial goals were somewhat unique, they still carry a 'dream' feeling. Napoleon Hill said a goal is a dream with a deadline. Adding a date to the objective enhances the sense of urgency. Moreover, it promotes discipline, one of the indispensable ingredients to achieving success. This brings us to the second component of setting a goal.

Step II: Set a deadline

Do you remember the first time you had to do homework for school in first grade? Most likely, you do not. If you do, you are an incredible person and I would love to meet you. Nonetheless, we can all agree on the fact that nine out of ten times, there was a deadline and you had to submit it to your teacher the next day or a few days later. From the very first days of our academic careers, we were programmed to expect homework, assignments and papers with a deadline. Now that we've reached our professional careers, we are also faced with due dates. If you are an accountant, April 15 is a major deadline for you. If you are a project manager, you live by deadlines. Even in sales, the end of a quarter is a serious deadline to meet goals in order to obtain earned incentives. When are football or soccer games the most exciting and

energetic? When there are just a few minutes remaining on the scoreboard and one team must score to win the game. So, when it comes to our financial goals, it is important to apply the same mindset.

Let's take the financial goals mentioned previously and let's add a date to their definition.

- **By December 31st of this year**, I will have $5,000 saved.

- Next year, I will need a new car. I will finance no more than $20,000 and I will have at least $4,000 saved as a down payment **by the end of March**.

- We currently have four credit cards. We will pay off **one each year** for the next three years so that we only have one with a balance **by 2019**.

- I have been saving about $400 every month and I will double that amount **in exactly one year.**

When I do this exercise with my millennial clients, from the corner of their mouth I see a smile start to form up. Before, it was a great idea, but now the goal is an aspiration we can strategize about. The difference is that there is an end-date to it. From the time Heather and I combined our finances, every year in December, we have mapped out our financial goals for the following twelve months. Whether it is an increase to our salary or a number of dollars to be saved, we define it, we agree upon it and set a deadline for it. It is an indescribable blessing for any man to know that he has a partner who has his back, who trusts him and locks efforts to achieve a common goal. Dear friends, I can see the wheels running through your mind asking how can goals get achieved if they are just written on a piece of paper. We will get into the 'how' in the next chapters, but setting a goal with a deadline is the inevitable starting point. As Tony Robbins said 'Setting goals is the first step in turning the invisible into the visible'.

Step III: See it every day, multiple times

I told you earlier that Heather and I always set our yearly goals in December. We not only define and set them, we write them down. Then we post the pieces of paper in places where see the goals multiple times a day. Last year when we decided on our savings objective, Heather wrote the dollar amount on a piece of paper with a marker then proceeded to laminate it and make it her bookmark. When you enter our home, and take a glance at our refrigerator, you will see some of our goals taped to the door. In our office, it is written on a white board and in our bedroom, I have it in a photo frame sitting on my nightstand. I also have my goals written on a laminated piece of paper which I keep in my vehicle and read it several times. I came home one evening to find some of our goals written on the mirror in the bathroom.

I'd rather be different than worried about being able to pay my bills. I'd rather be 'weird' than penalized with a bad credit score.

In any endeavor, succeeding requires an elevated amount of focus. That focus cannot be sustained if the pursuant does not constantly remind themselves of their goal. Is it radical? It may be, but I'd rather be different than worried about being able to pay my bills. I'd rather be 'weird' than penalized with a bad credit score. When your friends come over, I can guarantee you that there will be some raised eyebrows. There will be some talk behind your back. Remember that those who criticize you for being 'different' wish deep inside that they could be as determined as you. Let them talk. So be it. Great achievements are accomplished by those who dare to be different. I can also guarantee you that your radical stand will be an inspiration for others around you. Millennials, if standing out of the pack and being given looks is the price to pay to have peace of mind, then we must be willing and excited to look at the masses and do the opposite, the uncomfortable.

Pablo Picasso said: 'Our goals can only be reached through a vehicle of a plan, in which we must fervently believe, and upon which we must vigorously act. There is no other route to success'.

It is time to act!

Chapter III: It's time to create a budget

You know the big-ticket expenses in your life, but all the smaller spending can also be a killer. Take a look at your monthly outflow, and I guarantee you will have a few "Yikes, I had no idea" moments. - Suze Orman

In 2015, Melanie's salary was $45,000. Factor in the wonderful Uncle Sam taxes and as a single girl, she netted about $38,000. Here we are in July, it's close to the end of the month, she has thankfully paid her rent and she is about to overdraw her checking account. She starts thinking. It's soon August, which means she has already made more than $22,000 this year but, her bank says she has absolutely nothing. Melanie

Would you invest in You, Inc. today?

has worked a few extra hours this past week to make some overtime income, but where did it all go? Well, for many of us millennials, a large chunk of our money goes towards food. Per Gallup, people 18 to 29 spend an average of $173 per week on food and those 30 to 49 years old spend an average of one 167[1]. Interestingly, people making $75,000 or more reported spending $180, only about ten dollars more than millennials whose median income is $35,000[2].

Imagine a corporation which does not have a budget and accounting staff. There are no exact figures for revenues, expenses, profits and assets. Nobody knows whether the corporation is dramatically losing or succeeding. Would you invest in such a corporation? The answer is a big NO. Just like a corporation, you are a financial entity. Let's call you 'You, Inc.' You, Inc. is an entity with revenues and expenses. Would you invest in You, Inc. today?

Knowing how your income is spent is essential to managing it well and efficiently. In fact, Bankrate.com says that failure to set up a budget is the number one financial mistake millennials make[3]. For Heather and I, using a budget was one of the best decisions we'd ever made in regards to our money.

The How

This portion of *Money-Smart Millennials* is very technical. It requires your participation. If you are not a numbers person and do not care about mathematics at all, you will still be able to accomplish the task. However, this is not about downloading an app from Google Play or the Apple Store. Those are useful tools. Nonetheless,

I have not found one that reminds you that your student loan payment is due in two days and advises you not to buy the new pair of Jordan's. The purpose of the technique I am about to show you is to give you the tools to make adjustments in order to reach the goals you have written down. Unless you've generated a passive income stream for yourself, you've worked to make your money. You were active for eight, nine, ten or twelve hours of your day for weeks. Millennial,

Our generation is known to quit too early and to be distracted too easily. Let's prove them wrong. Use your goals as your motivation and be determined to reach the finish line.

you must be active with the management of your finances too. Financial stability is not passive. It does not happen by accident. So, let's get started.

Using Microsoft Excel or in your Google sheets, create a spreadsheet with 5 columns and 33 rows. From the left to the right in the first row, name the columns as follows: Monthly Bills, Due Date, Amount Due, Balance, and Paid. Under Monthly Bills, write Starting Balance. Then from the third row under the Due Date column, insert in the cells the numbers 1 through 31 matching the row numbers. Add colors at your own discretion. Here is an example.

Monthly Bills	Due Date	Amount Due	Balance	Paid
Starting Balance				
	1			
	2			
	3			
	4			
	5			
	6			
	7			
	8			
	9			
	10			
	11			
	12			
	13			
	14			
	15			
	16			
	17			
	18			
	19			
	20			
	21			
	22			
	23			
	24			

	25			
	26			
	27			
	28			
	29			
	30			
	31			

On a separate sheet of paper, write down a list of every single bill you pay each month. Next, write on the same sheet of paper the amount of your weekly, biweekly or monthly paycheck. If you are paid hourly, compute the average of your past 8 regular paychecks and jot down that figure. Notice here that we are considering your regular paycheck. If you were sick for two days during a certain week or worked overtime, do not consider that paystub.

Bills
Rent
Car Insurance
YMCA membership
Bank of America credit card
Amex card
Netflix
Phone bill
Electricity bill
Water bill

Paul School loan payment
Jess school loan payment
Paul's car loan payment
Jess' car loan payment
Cable bill
Internet bill

<u>*Paycheck*</u>
Paul: 1st and 15th of the month -
$1457
Jess: Fridays biweekly - $1290

Let's go back to the spreadsheet and add the monthly bills (and their corresponding amounts) and your paychecks in accordance to their respective date of the month. If your pay dates vary each month as you are remunerated every other Friday for example, determine which dates they would fall on next month. Your spreadsheet should now be similar to the following. Good job!

Monthly Bills	Due Date	Amount Due	Balance	Paid
Starting Balance				
Paul's paycheck	1			
	2			
	3			
Rent	4			
Car Insurance	5			
Jess' paycheck	6			
YMCA membership	7			
Netflix	8			
	9			
Phone bill	10			
	11			
BOA credit card	12			
Paul's car loan payment	13			
	14			
Paul's paycheck	15			
Internet bill	16			
	17			
AMEX	18			

credit card				
Electricity	19			
Jess' paycheck	20			
	21			
Jess' car loan payment	22			
	23			
Cable	24			
	25			
	26			
Water bill	27			
Paul's school loan payment	28			
	29			
	30			
	31			

You should be starting to see how your finances play out each month. There are still a few steps leading to the full picture. The time has come to input dollar amounts. For the Microsoft Excel novice or Google Spreadsheet amateur, feel free to get help on this step. We are not all the meticulous type; so, going into so much detail may not be your cup of tea. I do understand. However, I encourage you to be persistent and finish the task. Our generation is known to quit too early and to be distracted too easily. Let's prove them wrong. Use your goals as your motivation and be determined to reach the finish line. In your spreadsheet, in the cell under Balance, enter the dollar amount in your checking account at the beginning of the month. Below that amount, we will enter the following formula: *sum of the cell above and the cell of the bill*. Press Enter then drag the formula all the way down to the last cell in the Balance column.

Monthly Bills	Due Date	Amount Due	Balance	Paid
Starting Balance			756	
Paul's paycheck	1	1430	2186 (F6)	X
Medical bill	2	-50 (E7)	=sum(F6+E7)	X

In the 'Paid' column, enter a X next to the specific bill once you have paid it.

Now you have a better understanding of your overall finances. Did this step totally go over your head? Do not worry, you are still in the race. Feel free to use the budget I have designed for you. I invite you to visit subscribe to *Money-Smart Millennials* website at www.moneysmartmillennials.com. Click on the 'Budget Template' page and simply request access to download the file. It already has the formula computed.

Let's now add the various expenses which do not necessarily fall under a bill category. They may be fuel expenses, lunch, groceries, etc. Go ahead and add a row for savings. This may be at the beginning of the month, at the end of a month, or a couple of times per month according to your personal situation. Before I show you how to input these expenses into your budget, let's do a quick-thinking exercise together.

The indispensable expenses

Expenditures such as fuel, lunch food, groceries, public transportation for some of us, etc. are inevitable. We know they're coming and we also know how much they cost. So why not plan for them? Heather and I have found that being specific about these expenses have saved us thousands of dollars over the years. We have incorporated them into our budget and chosen to regard them as bills which have due dates.

1. Fuel expense: A few years ago, I figured that I was spending about $30 in gas every week. That was about a full tank of gas for

my Nissan Sentra sedan. Heather had a longer commute than I did, so her cost was about $50. We decided that we were going to get respectively $30 and $50 of fuel once a week, even if we ended up not fully filling the tank. Could we have gotten more? Of course, we could have. However, it allowed us to input this into our budget and more importantly, it gave us a sense of where our bank account would stand every time we got fuel in our tanks. At the time, we had just gotten married and our money was quite tight. Figure out how much your weekly commute costs you. Whether you are driving or utilizing public transportation, there must be a fixed cost. Next, choose a day to input it in your budget. For us, it was Sundays.

2. Lunches: How much money do you spend for food every day? This includes breakfast, lunch and snacks. If you are like the average millennial in today's America, you are buying between $20 and $25 worth of food every day. In other words, your weekly food 'bill' is approximately one $140 and up to $175. Just as you did for your fuel expense, pick a day of the

week to insert this bill in your budget. You must determine a specific amount for your or your household. Once you have a number, my suggestion is to withdraw that amount from your checking account on the day which you chose for your budget. Then leave your apartment or house daily with $25 in cash and spend no more on food.

How do we add these expenses to the budget? Simple. Once you have elected the day to get cash from your checking account for food, refer to a calendar for the specific date of the month which corresponds to your day. Then insert a new row in your budget for that specific 'bill'. Eventually, you will have the same day of the month for multiple bills.

This step of creating a budget is simple, but not easy. Creating this budget on a regular basis will require time, dedication and persistence. Make time to edit your budget for the upcoming month(s). More importantly, set aside a time slot to review it on a regular basis. Unexpected

Being financially fit requires dedicated time and discipline. We must remember that motivation only gets us going but discipline keeps us going.

purchases happen and when they do, you will need to add those debits to your budget. That is where discipline is a factor. Dear friends, any worthwhile accomplishment in life demands discipline. Anyone who aims at being physically fit must not only set a time to exercise, but also maintain consistency at it. Similarly, being financially fit requires dedicated time and discipline. We must remember that motivation only gets us going, but discipline keeps us going. James Allen said: 'Men are anxious to improve their circumstances, but are unwilling to improve themselves; they therefore remain bound.' Don't let that be you. Ask yourself: am I ok with what my financial picture will be if I don't build a budget and create discipline? Ultimately, this budget is your step to financial stability.

Chapter IV: Your budget is your financial GPS

You were born to win, but to be a winner you must plan to win, prepare to win and expect to win. - Zig Ziglar

Kyle and Jessica were trying to save an additional $300 every month. Their breakfast and lunch budget was $800 meaning $20 each, every work day of the month. They decided to reduce their monthly eating out budget by $200, an amount which would go towards the goal. Instead of spending $20 daily, they would only spend $15 for lunch. For breakfast, they decided to eat at home, adding a mere weekly $15 ($60 per month) to their grocery budget. They had figured out how to save an extra $140. They also have a $100 per month gym membership which included a $25 fee for group classes. After being members for two years, they had only attended one class.

Consequently, the decision to drop the unnecessary fee, which now brought their savings to an additional $165 monthly, was very

Most debtors or creditors will allow you to move your due date at your convenience at least once or twice during the life of the loan.

easy. Working and strategizing together, they eventually came to a game plan that added $350 extra to their savings.

Another client of mine, Anita, a 30-year-old music teacher had a $315 car payment due on the 22nd of the month. She would usually make the payment on the 20th or 21st. Then on the 30th, her $1200 rent payment would be due preceded by a $125 car and rental insurance bill on the 25th and her student loan payment on the 27th. She would then receive her paycheck on the 1st day of the following month, usually short after her checking account was empty or had been withdrawn and penalized with non-sufficient funds (NSF) fees. Anita's challenge was that the bulk of her bills was all due in the second half of the month and in the span of one week. To create a balance in her budget for better management, I suggested rearranging her bills. Most debtors or creditors will allow you to move your due date at your convenience at least once or twice during the life of the loan. Take advantage of that option if it's beneficial to you. Anita contacted her car note lender, her insurance company and her student loan administrator and was able to move those due dates to the first half of the month. Although it did not change the amount she owed every month, it reduced her stress which was her ultimate goal.

I give you these two examples to show how

by utilizing your budget, you will be able to unveil the hidden opportunities in your finances. I once heard successful entrepreneur Matt Grotewold illustrate it as follows. During a road trip, when you deviate from the route the GPS has chosen, it recalculates your itinerary using algorithms, getting you to the destination. Your financial goal is the desired destination. You do not have to come up with an algorithm for your financial goal, but you do have in your budget an effective tool that plays the same role. Maximize that tool and you will achieve your goal by incrementally improving your finances every month.

When Heather and I first implemented this technique, it was exciting to feel and be in control of our expenses and assets. It wasn't perfect at the beginning, but we kept at it. This

The point is not to have such a specific personal budget for the rest of your life, but to manage your money well enough today so that tomorrow, you live comfortably and without stress.

happened over five years ago. Today, our finances are in a much better place and consequently, we have become more flexible. As our income increased, our savings grew as well. Nowadays, I can get away with gratifying myself with a new toy purchase without feeling guilty. 'Do you then still follow a budget?' you may ask. Absolutely! Why? Because Heather and I have a bigger goal, more important than a 55'' smart TV. You may be thinking that you do not need a budget because you make enough money. That might very well be the case. The point is not to have such a specific personal budget for the rest of your life, but to manage your money well enough today so that tomorrow, you live comfortably and without stress. Trust me, you will discover something about your finances that you haven't realized. Let me illustrate.

Rachel is a 26-year-old software engineer in Bethesda, MD whose salary is $72,000. Her goal is to be a homeowner by 2021 and she wants to have $60,000 saved for her down payment. Being a single girl and living with two roommates, it turned out that saving $15,000 ($1,250/month) each year for the next four years was not a terrifying challenge. With her income, Rachel was not hurt by eating out four or five times a week. Nonetheless, every time I met with her, she would complain about being behind on her goal. Somehow, when the 30th of the month came, Rachel would not be able to transfer the desired amount to her savings account. So, I shared the budget technique with her. It looked great and we were both excited. However, there was an issue. Rachel did not incorporate her shopping habits. Together, we realized that

Rachel was spending at least an extra $150 every month shopping at department stores and sometimes upwards of $400. Rachel loved shopping for new clothes on a regular basis. At an average of $200 per month, she was delaying her savings goal by $2,400 a year buying clothing and accessories. It did not seem like much to her monthly, but once we computed the yearly expenditure, she concluded that she did not need to spend so much on clothing. That was a huge chunk out her income. Here is the game plan we created. Every month, she would transfer to her savings the planned $1,250 plus any additional money sitting in her checking account that she did not need. Then every fourth month, she would withdraw $500 from her savings and go enjoy herself shopping. The result: she spent $1,500 on clothing that first year implementing a budget thus keeping $900 that she would have easily lost without even realizing. When you decide to use your budget as your guide, just like Heather and I had to figure out, you will find areas of improvement as you keep consistent. It's an inevitable part of the process. In any endeavor in life, I have learned in my only twenty-eight years of existence that it takes many failures to achieve worthwhile success. Do not be discouraged if you stumble upon difficulties and setbacks. I assure you that it is normal.

Part II

Downtown Frederick, MD by Lionel Hounkanrin

A survey was conducted asking millennials this question: 'Do you wish you had practical money management education in school?'. Only about 2% of the participants responded no. Some were indifferent, but the majority wanted some type of education on money management. In the same survey, the respondents were asked to describe their go-to tactic in overseeing their finances. More than 70% admitted that they only check their account balances on somewhat of a regular basis. And dear friends, that is the reason why I have to reject multiple requests for Non-Sufficient Funds fees waivers on a daily basis at the bank. I made the same mistake in the past and I know what it feels like when you have to pay extra fees when your account is already overdrawn. Unfortunately for the consumer, this type of fee is a major revenue generator for the banks and they would rarely waive it. Nonetheless, let's take responsibility for our actions. The banks are not the ones to blame when we have already consumed our purchases. As harsh as it may sound, if your financial

If your financial decisions are only determined by the balance in your bank account at a specific time, I am not sorry to break the news to you: you will never have enough money to be financially stable.

decisions are only determined by the balance in your bank account at a specific time, I am not sorry to break the news to you: you will never have enough money to be financially stable.

The following chapters will present to you tips and mindset that have helped many millennials reach financial stability. It is not rocket science; in fact, it is very simple. I've chosen a few tips focusing on the mistakes that I've seen tons of millennials make, myself included. I've learned from them and I hope you avoid them.

It takes personal desire to achieve your financial goal, but most importantly, it takes discipline and delayed gratification. It also takes adopting a different decision-making pattern. The truth is that your current financial position is the result of a decision-making system you have applied in your life. Whether it was taught to you by your parents or peers or whether you have constructed it yourself, it is yours to take the responsibility to steer your financial decision-making process in a different direction if it has not brought you desired results.

Chapter I: Banking, debt and credit

Rather go to bed without dinner than to rise in debt. - Benjamin Franklin

'No' for overdrafts

About nine years ago, I had an experience that I will probably never forget. It's not because it was an incredible and exciting experience, but it is because my pride took a serious hit. Younger 19-year-old Lionel had overdrawn his checking account

Millennials, my recommendation is to always 'opt-out'.

with two transactions. I spent 30 minutes on the phone with the bank customer service representative trying to get him to waive the $70 fees. As if I had some type of authority over him and as if I was entitled to get the fee waived, I even requested that he put his manager on the line so that I could complain. What a humiliating picture! How annoyed that employee would've been while talking to me! Here we are nine years later and I am working for that same bank. I am now the one so fed up with clients requesting refunds. It so baffles me when people deliberately choose to 'opt-in' for overdrafts on their checking account when they obviously struggle with money management. Millennials, my recommendation is to always 'opt-out'. By applying the budget technique that I have shown you, you will know when the balance in your account is very low. In addition, nowadays many financial institutions offer mobile alerts for your accounts. Take advantage of what's offered to you. If you're not sure at the time of a purchase, simply check your balance. Why pay $35 when you overdraw your account by $2? Many consumers don't even know which overdraft election is set up with their checking account. If you are trying to get on your feet financially, you cannot afford to pay unnecessary NSF fees. You might as well throw money out of your car's windows while driving on the highway. Call your bank today and 'opt out'.

Consolidate your debt

Rick and Sam, a married couple in their late 20's, were paying over $550 in credit card bills every month. With the astonishingly high interest rates on the cards, only approximately $425 was being applied to the principal.

Although they were slowly getting ahead, they hated seeing so much money wasted every month. A simple Google search for '0% balance transfer credit cards' led to transferring $7500 to a new credit card with a very small transfer fee and 0% APR for 18 months. Continuing to pay $550 per month, Rick and Sam allocated more than $1800 to their credit card principal even before the promotion ended. How cool is that?! Very. This would not have happened if they kept the initial high interest credit card. For you, the solution may be getting an unsecured loan. An unsecured loan will keep your monthly payment constant. A constant payment will allow you to budget better since it does not vary month to month. In addition, you will know that by a certain date, that specific debt will be paid off.

I would like to emphasize that this option may not be appropriate for everyone. Rick and Sam had good credit scores and they were not delinquent on their debt. They had never missed a due date. To my clients who have low credit scores and bad credit history, I recommend looking for savings elsewhere in their budget. An application for a new credit card would most likely be a wasted inquiry and a potential harm for their already affected score. It is also important to keep in mind that consolidation is worthless if you are not disciplined afterwards. Make it a point to pay off your purchases or do not use that credit card at all. Rick and Sam came back to my office once they received the new credit card, chopped it up right there and did not order a new one until it had an outstanding balance of zero dollars.

Your car is paid for, keep it for a few years

When my first car loan was finally paid in full a few years ago, I decided to keep it for a while before purchasing a new vehicle. During those years, Heather and I changed the car loan payment on our budget into a transfer to our savings account. Lo and behold just a year later, we had added $3000 to our savings. The figure in our account was so encouraging that 3 years later, I was

> *Status is buying things you can't afford to impress people who do not care.*

still driving the same car knowing that we had saved over $10,000 during that period. My Nissan Sentra was still in good condition and it did not require constant maintenance.

Driving a new vehicle every five or six years may be an exciting experience. However, ask yourself: Am I buying a new car for myself or because I want to have status among my friends and acquaintances? In many cases, due to the influence of social circles, people buy new cars, new phones, new electronic gadgets or new clothes to keep up with the Joneses. When this becomes your practice, it could destroy your finances. Remember that status is simply buying things you can't afford to impress people who do not care. If your automobile is in very bad shape and needs to be replaced, it makes sense to invest into a new one especially if regular repairs become very expensive.

If you have to get a loan or set up a payment plan for that entertainment system, you can't afford it right now

Study.com defines delayed gratification as the ability to put off something mildly fun or pleasurable now, in order to gain something that is more fun, pleasurable, or rewarding later[1]. We live in a society of instant gratification; a world of microwave cooking, drive-thru restaurants and Google searches. When we miss an exit on the highway, the GPS automatically

Dear fellow millennials, when it comes to money management, we must delay that feeling of gratification and exercise self-control.

readjusts to lead us to the same destination. We post pictures of new babies from the hospital because the world must know with no delay that Johnny is born. By the way, we wanted to stream his birth live but the nurse declined our request. As millennials, we have been programmed to expect everything to be immediate and available instantly. Dear fellow millennials, when it comes to money management, we must delay that feeling of gratification and exercise self-control. I counsel with clients and this is usually their thought process. When they can make the monthly payments comfortably on a purchase such as an entertainment system, they assume that they can afford it. However, the right perspective is very contrary. A major component of financial stability is having a substantial amount of savings which would cover a minimum of six months' worth of expenses. If you are not able to save money because you must make payments on your wireless speakers, you truly cannot afford those fancy speakers now. Delay that gratification. Be patient and disciplined with your budget. I promise you that the day will come when you will purchase those speakers in one payment and still have plenty of reserves.

I sincerely wish that there was a course on delayed gratification in our schools. It will serve us all well.

Take advantage of credit unions for your lending needs

In general, credit unions will offer you a lower interest rate than major banks on loans. According to BankRate, they will also charge you lower fees than most banks[2]. Although they do restrain access to their services with membership eligibility requirements, many credit unions are very flexible. You may be able to qualify for membership through your employer, your school, your community, your social affiliations or through your family relations. Search for a local credit union and join even it is just to get a better rate on your car loan or mortgage.

Arrange a change of payment due date with your lender

I previously mentioned Anita, the 30-year-old music teacher and how she called her lender to change the due date on her car note payment. This is a practice to take advantage of if you find yourself struggling to pay too many bills in a very short length of time, i.e. a week or less. When Marcelo, a semi-pro soccer player had a surgery to fix a recent sports injury, he had to assume a new bill every month for the next three years. His car payment was due on the 5th and the hospital bill on the 8th. He could afford both, but just like Anita, his finances would then be very tight until he got paid again on the 15th of the month. Marcelo called the bank which owned his car loan and they allowed him to move his payment due date to the 16th, right after his direct deposit hit his checking account on the 15th of the month.

What can you do when your lender does not offer you this option? There is another solution. Years ago, while working a minimum wage job, even before I knew about the practice of changing your due dates, here is how I managed my budget. My car note was $208 due on the 25th of the month. I would make a payment of $104 at the beginning of the month and later, submit the other half after my second paycheck. This worked perfectly with my finances and I never had a past due bill.

Set up a meeting with your banker

Yes, an in-person meeting. Technology advances are molding us into the most anti-social generation, but interaction is still needed when your personal finances and future are at stake. In the several years that I have worked in the banking industry, I rarely encounter a millennial who takes the initiative to meet with me or another banker to discuss their banking and finances. Why wait until the years close to an important purchase or investment or retirement to become serious about your money? It will be too late. Remember that a champion is not made in the ring, he is just recognized there. The training grind happens when all the doors are closed and no one is watching.

You may think that your account is worthless to a banker because you only keep a few hundred dollars in it. If a banker would not meet with you for that reason, it is time to break up with that bank. Make the point to discuss and preferably to meet with a bank representative at least once a year. The objective in discussing with your banker is to identify areas of opportunities for your finances.

Have you been paying monthly service charges? Banks make a ton of profit by charging maintenance fees. In general, checking accounts are designed with requirements to meet to avoid a certain monthly fee. Whether it is $5 or $25, it is money wasted when you pay them. Find out which checking account will match your usage to avoid paying a fee and stick to it. I personally favor the ones that require a direct deposit. As long as you are working and are being remunerated, you are safe. Just make sure that you set up a direct deposit with your employer instead of receiving checks. Some accounts require you to maintain an average monthly minimum balance. Be aware that this average minimum balance is computed based on your statement cycle which may not be from the first of the month to the thirtieth. Unless, you are certain that you will maintain a minimum amount in your checking (or savings) account, go with the easier option to avoid maintenance charges.

Is the interest rate on your credit card too high? The goal is to get out of debt. While you are on your way to meeting that goal, let's avoid throwing away your hard-earned money into the high interest rate waste basket. I mentioned earlier how to consolidate your debt. Your banker may be able to help by identifying the best solution(s).

Are you missing out on cash back rewards? If your finances are stable and in good standing, chances are that you are being offered countless credit cards. Be careful and do not fall for the temptation of accepting them all. But if you are going to select one, go with a company that offers cash back and/or other rewards. Unless you are spending tens of thousands of dollars monthly, your rewards may not be highly attractive, but you may still be able to treat yourself to a nice dinner occasionally. In my case, a couple years ago I combined the rewards on my cards and bought a DSLR camera.

Should you take advantage of promotional

interest rates on savings accounts?
Alright, go ahead and laugh. Interest rates on savings accounts are a joke in today's world. I know. As a

banker, I used to detest having to deal with those clients who live to rate-shop. I would work hard at convincing them to open an account with me only to see them close it a few months later and move the funds to another institution. But then I realized, it was their money and they had the right to do whatever they wanted with it. Plus, if they could get a bit more in interest elsewhere it made sense to break the relationship with me. After all, their loyalty to me would not pay their bills. Millennials, do not count on your deposit accounts for any substantial return. Nonetheless, do take advantage of rates especially when they are competitive. I have found that banks which offer online accounts usually have higher promotional and regular rates on their savings accounts. It might be worth considering.

These are just a few topics to discuss with a banker. One very important point to keep in mind is that not all bankers are equal. The quality of their advice will relatively match their experience and their willingness to honestly help you. So, if you feel like your banker could be doing a better job or is not an expert on a particular issue, take action. It is not rude to request an expert when the subject of the discussion obviously matters to you; just make sure that you are not impolite, impatient or ill-mannered.

Chapter II: Make money-smart choices

The choices you make now, the people you surround yourself with, they all have the potential to affect your life, even who you are, forever. - Sarah Dessen

Avoid paying for unnecessary insurance and/or services

In a conversation with Mark, a former colleague, he mentioned that he was paying an extra $15 per month for a cell phone insurance plan. If his phone were to drop into the toilet, his service provider would replace it contingent on a $199 deductible. Considering that the retail price for his 64GB Samsung Galaxy S6 was $650, I first thought this may be a very good idea. Then I asked Mark how many times he's had to replace a phone because it was damaged. He replied once or twice in the fifteen years that he's been using mobile phones. The probability of Mark damaging his phone and needing a replacement was very slim. Essentially, Mark was wasting $180 per year.

The average lifespan of a laptop computer today is five years. Squaretrade would offer you a 3-year insurance plan at a rate of $289 for your $700 laptop[1]. Again, it's not a bad deal, but I've had an HP laptop for 6 years and I've never dropped it, hit it or spilled coffee on it. I worked hard to earn the money to buy it, so I'm careful in the way I handle it. My message is that with some care on my part, such a service is unnecessary for me. For you also, it may not be needed. So why pay for it?

Before we move to the next tip, I would like to clarify that I am not advocating a boycott of these services or types of insurance. I am sure that some of us need cell phone or computer insurance, have benefited from it and should subscribe to some type of protection. What is best for you? You decide.

Buy quality, not cheap

There was a time when I confused getting a good deal to buying cheap. I would spend $6 on a shirt and congratulate myself for saving a lot of money. Then a few weeks later, I would have to go shopping again because the shirt was damaged either from use or wash. Many individuals think the same way, convinced that they cannot afford to shop quality items. The reality is that you cannot afford not to if you are trying to establish stable finances. I've learned that it is more economical to spend $40 on a shirt which will last years than to spend $15 on one which will need to be replaced 3 times in one year. I made the same mistake while shopping for tires and other maintenance services on my vehicle a few years ago. Another time, my car was hit in a parking lot. After getting the $500 check from the insurance company, I figured that my friend's father who had a 'shop' in his garage would easily fix my alignment issues for just a couple hundred dollars. Bad idea. Soon enough, a professional garage charged me more than $500 for the same problems. In all, I

Saving does not mean going for low quality items.

ended up spending almost a thousand dollars for a mechanical issue which could had been solved for much less. Saving does not mean going for low quality items. Millennials, when you shop, find great quality and invest in it within measures and your buying power. You will look great, feel better and save a lot of your money long term.

Be accountable

Once you have decided to work towards

your goal, there is a flame of motivation burning inside of you. You see the end of the tunnel becoming a reality and your belief drives your determination and discipline. I've learned that the best way to keep that motivation strong is to share your goal with someone who trusts you, believes in you and whom you respect. Then commit to be accountable to your goal and to this individual. Their job is to ensure that you do not give up on your objective or deviate from the path that leads to your financial stability. It must be important to you to not disappoint this person. They may be a parent or a friend; regardless of who they are, your accountability partner must be willing to stand firm and tell you when are wrong.

Do you have such an accountability partner in your life in regards to your finances? Heather and I have used this tip since the beginning of our relationship. It will certainly play out differently for everyone but for us, it simply meant agreeing on certain purchases and financial decisions before they were done. If you are married or in a serious relationship, I recommend taking a leap of faith. Discuss with your partner and establish your accountability parameters. It could simply be letting the other person know when a purchase of $50 or more outside of your established budget is about to happen. You can choose what you are comfortable with. I can't honestly admit to you

how many times I have gotten very excited
about something and been ready to purchase it
only to be brought to my senses by Heather, and
vice versa.

Establish your money management
philosophy

In November of 2011, when I told my friend
and mentor Michael that I was going to propose
to Heather, we had a long talk; a talk that I
would never forget. We discussed marriage,
accountability, responsibility, honor, my
relationship with my God and its impact on my
future marriage. We also discussed finances and
the importance of having a 'money management
philosophy' in my household. What is your
decision-making process when it comes to
money? Do you believe in saving? Do you
believe in giving back? Are you an investor? Are
you a gambler? What is your mentality on loans
and credit? Do you believe in setting up a life
insurance policy? Michael advised me to have
these important discussions with Heather
because it will later determine the direction of
our family in terms of finances. It is one of the
best pieces of advice that I have ever received. I
am not sure if it was custom for older
generations to have these types of conversations
(although I am certain that my own parents once

did, but I can guarantee that not many millennials care to establish a money management philosophy. A few years ago, at a leadership conference, I was listening to author John Maxwell when he said that leaders must set their standards before they are faced with a difficult decision. In the same way, having a set mindset on money management will allow you to make the right choice when faced with a financial issue or dilemma. Heather and I did so years ago and I can tell you that it has saved us countless arguments. Moreover, it let us come to a common ground on how we wanted to manage our money as a couple and as a family. A simple example is that we decided that we would combine our finances, we would make financial decisions together and we would agree on all major expenditures before they were consumed. I am not advocating that you should make the same choice for your family. However, I am urging you to define your philosophy and live by it. Through the years, I have witnessed many interesting discussions in my office while meeting with clients at the bank. After being married for a year, Shawn and Melissa came to my office to apply for a new car loan. Shawn's car had just been paid off and he wanted a new one. On the other side, Melissa thought that they should wait a few years and save the money. They had never had a conversation on the topic until Shawn's bachelor car was paid in full and it was obvious that Melissa did not agree with her husband and did not want to be there in my office. The question of deciding on your financial philosophy does not only apply to couples. If you are single, decide today how to make financial decisions with your money.

Get proper exposure and advice

Five years from now, you will be in a position in life based on your closest network and the books that you read today. Notice that I did not say the friends that you have on Facebook or Instagram. Nor did I say the entertainment videos that you watch on YouTube or the blogs that you read on Google. Your associations and the content of what you cultivate your mind with has a big impact on your financial literacy. In addition, in five years, your financial strength or lack thereof will be the average of the five people that you spend the most time with. In fact, think about the friends that you hang around the most today and I can guarantee you that your income is very close to theirs or in the same tax bracket. Here is my point: to get where you want to be financially, you must thrive to spend time with people who are in life where you want to end up. Be aware that you must make some tough decisions at times. When your friends decide to go to the beach and waste away all their savings, it may not be the right time for you to tag along. When you start networking with social groups or individuals who are in life where you want to be, those who do not aim for anything will criticize you for not spending all your time with them anymore. You must also educate yourself on principles of financial stability and success which unfortunately, are not taught in our system of education.

> *Millennials, our financial future is a matter of such importance that we cannot afford to make decisions solely based on opinions. We must get factual and credible advice.*

Very often, while discussing with my clients I ask them how they make their financial decisions. In general, most millennials refer to their friends, parents and the internet. To get them thinking, I usually present them this case and let them respond. Imagine that you were about to buy a luxurious sports vehicle and you had narrowed your choices down to the Ferrari F12Berlinetta and the Lamborghini Huracan. Across the street from your house is a Honda automotive shop where your longtime friend Alex works. However, five miles down the road is a luxurious car dealership which also has a maintenance shop with a handful of experts on Ferrari and Lamborghini. Would you call Alex or drive down to the car dealership to get advice from an expert on which car to purchase? 100% of the time, the answer is the second option. I hope you made the same choice. Though Alex may gladly instruct you on his mindset, his recommendations will be nothing but opinions. In this situation, you must make a logical decision. You may be the most emotional person who has walked this earth, but this particular choice must be logical and intelligent. It has nothing to do with your friendship with Alex and hopefully Alex understands and does not resent you. You must treat your money with the same attitude.

Millennials, our financial future is a matter of such importance that we cannot afford to make decisions solely based on opinions. We must get factual and credible advice.

Give back

Giving back can be a controversial and sensitive topic. For some, it would be a religious matter while for others it would be a spiritual one. There are also those for whom the concept of giving back is a simple moral obligation and finally, some of us millennials do not care. In my opinion, giving must be a volunteer act meant to better the life or the circumstances of others. I would not attempt here to convince you to give away to your communities. Nonetheless, I would tell you that as I experienced, when we take our eyes off ourselves, we realize that our financial struggles may not be as severe as the hardship of others. While the unfortunate may benefit from our financial gifts, we are the ones who are truly uplifted by the feeling of helping someone else.

'No-one has ever become poor by giving', did say Anne Frank. I love John Wesley's advice: 'Make all you can, save all you can, give all you can.'

'You can have everything in life you want, if you will just help other people get what they want.' I personally believe this is also true: 'When you help enough people get what they need, you will also receive what you need.'

In addition to the indescribable feeling which one gets from helping others, my personal experience is that the forces of this world work in mysterious ways to bring back tenfold what an honest and willing heart gives. As Christians, Heather and I allocate a portion of our income to giving back to organizations and ministries we strongly believe in.

As a 19-year-old working a minimum wage

job, I am still amazed today at how I somehow managed to pay for out-of-state tuition but I did. With such a small income averaging $700 biweekly, I would tithe and give away sometimes $70 or more. Then in unexpected ways, it would be returned to me multiplied like the evening I found out about a scholarship Frederick Community College was offering. It was the last day to submit applications which consisted of a written paper. I applied and a few weeks later, I was awarded a grant toward my tuition.

Do you have $5 or $10 to spare every week or every month? Start there. Choose an organization whose work you believe in and go ahead and support them. You might see blessings come back to you. Heck, if you don't, at least you would have done a good deed. Giving back also develops in you a habit and financial discipline.

If you're not sure which organization you should help, ask yourselves these questions:

- What am I passionate about?

- What makes me very compassionate?

- What do I value the most?

- What are the social needs in my community?

- How can I help millennials in struggling communities around the world?

- How much am I willing to donate?

Respond to these questions and find organizations that do work related to the answers to your questions. Then use your best judgement to select an organization that demonstrates credibility and integrity.

The late Zig Ziglar said: 'You can have everything in life you want, if you will just help other people get what they want'. I personally believe this is also true: 'When you help enough people get what they need, you will also receive what you need'.

Part III

Lincoln Memorial by Lionel Hounkanrin

In Part 1 and 2, we've learned how to organize our finances for more money to be kept rather than too much money leaving our households. Part 3 establishes the final component of financial stability: increasing your income. Let's face it, although poor money management is a pivotal source of financial instability, millennials are struggling even more because they simply do not make enough money.

I can vividly remember coming at a red light on a beautiful Monday morning in the fall 2008. It was 8 o'clock and I was heading to my job. I looked over to my left and it was obvious that the gentleman sitting in the car next to mine was not excited about going into work. It wasn't the first time that we've stopped at that light at the same time and as previously, the sadness in his face was depressing. Most mornings, I would guess the reason for his frown to entertain myself. 'Hates his job', 'just had a fight with the wife', 'working late today', 'has bills to pay', etc. were some of the theories I would come up with. But that Monday morning was different. To make sure that I didn't look like him, I glanced to my

> *'Things may come to those who wait, but only the things left behind by those who hustle.' Abraham Lincoln*

mirror to only realize that I also did not want to be at that red light, at that time of the day, on that exquisite fall morning. In fact, I was miserable. I had spent the whole night before worrying about my bills and how I would survive until I got paid. If you are in the same situation as I was then, you understand how frustrating and stressful that feeling is. That day and for the following week, I intensely thought about how I could increase my income. When an idea came to mind, I would write it down on a piece of paper and save it. By the end of the week, I had a handful of ideas to supplement my income and I was on my way to diversifying.

As millennials, we have a limitless number of opportunities to have multiple legal sources of income. Whether it is long-term or short-term, the goal is to generate the income necessary to reach financial stability. In the next few pages, I will give you tips and ways to diversify your income.

'Things may come to those who wait, but only the things left behind by those who hustle.'
Abraham Lincoln

Chapter I: Tips and mindset to have when it's time to increase your income

You can put someone in a new home, but you can't give them a new mindset. - Dan Phillips

Know what your number is

When I decided to diversify/increase my income, I needed an extra $500 per month to be comfortable. As a 20-year-old, and a student with such an increase in my budget, I could pay the few bills that I had and I had a few dollars left to save for entertainment. Today, things have changed in my life. In addition to my full-time job, my diversified income goal is much higher for Heather and I. Similarly, your budget and your desires will determine what the number is for you. How much would give you peace of mind? What amount of money would make you stress free about your finances? How much do you need to save every month that you are not currently saving? What will it take to replace your spouse's income? How much extra money will you need to take that cross-country trip you've always dreamt of? If you are looking to increase your household revenues, your starting point must be a defined goal.

Do not randomly pick a number as your goal. Be purposeful. Once you have your goal, then it is also important to identify how to achieve it. Your budget plays a key role in this process as well. Let's imagine that next summer, you would like to visit Ireland for two weeks. This is about ten months away. For the full experience and without any reserves, you were told by a travel agent that the vacation will cost you approximately $4000. That means that you should come up with $400 every month for the next ten. To go a step forward in the planning, your goal requires you to generate an extra $100 per week for the next ten weeks. What is easier to fathom? Come up with an extra $4000 over the next few months or make an extra $100 every week? Although they lead to the exact same goal, the latter plan seems more attainable.

Nobody becomes financially stable or wealthy by saving pennies

Have you ever heard the expression: 'Insanity is doing the same thing repeatedly and expecting different results'? I'm sure you have. I wouldn't recommend defining insanity as such in your psychiatry paper, but that definition does make a relevant point. I am incredibly baffled when I hear of or see people watching hours of the show 'Extreme Couponing'. Then they spend additional hours trying to collect coupons so that that they can save $50 on a grocery shopping trip. If your goal is to be financially sound, think outside of the box.

> *Being a money-smart millennial is more than savings money and finding great deals. It's finding the opportunities to maximize your revenues along with your savings.*

While one is 'working hard' for hours to save $50, one could deliver pizza in less time and make $150. Extreme couponing is simply 'insane'. In his article '*Sorry, But Saving Money Won't Make You Rich'*, Ben Walsh said it clearly and better that I could: '[...] household saving - whatever income people have left over after their spending - has little effect on boosting wealth.'[1] Wealth may not be your goal. If it is, I hope it's for the right reasons. Nonetheless, to be financially stable from your savings, you must think bigger than just couponing and going after deals. Being a money-smart millennial is more than saving money and finding great deals. It's finding the opportunities to maximize your revenues along with your savings.

When I needed to diversify my income, one

of my sources of revenue came from tutoring middle and high school students. Initially I was anxious of the fact that it may be a total failure. I was afraid that I would make mistakes and be rejected by the parents of my students. On the contrary, it was a great experience. I met some wonderful families who welcomed me in their homes and I was able to help those kids, but also help myself. At a rate of $45, $50 or $75 per hour, I would make hundreds of dollars on a weekly basis. Then Heather got on board and combined, we brought in so much that the revenues helped pay for a portion of our wedding expenses.

Define what you are willing to give up to attain your objective

Russ was deeply under water with his finances. His family was struggling to pay their mortgage on a consistent basis. As a former division one tennis player in college, he decided to coach an after-school program in his neighborhood to make some additional income. At first, it was a very exciting idea. The gig would surely generate enough to supplement Russ and his wife's incomes so that they could easily pay for the mortgage until things settled down. However, here is what Russ and Meg would sacrifice:

- An extra two hours of the day spent together

- Meg is a music teacher and often directs concerts with her students. Russ had never missed any of her performances, but taking on the tennis coaching gig, he would eventually have to be absent.

- Once a week, Russ would meet with his former college buddies for drinks. Now he wouldn't be able to do so.

Together Russ and Meg agreed that the results of his tennis coaching job are worth the sacrifices that they would make over a period. Is the result worth the sacrifice or the inconvenience for you? It may be or it may not quite be the right thing to do. Be wise in your decision. If you are giving up quantity and quality time with your young kids and family, I would suggest reconsidering.

Choose the opportunity that will generate the most amount of extra income in the shortest timeframe

Oprah Winfrey said: 'Real integrity is doing the right thing, knowing that nobody's going to know whether you did it or not.' When you go into your job every day, you are getting paid to perform for your employer. You have signed a contract with them. Be true to your employer and always demonstrate

Do the right thing.

honesty. It is not the place to edit the wedding pictures that you took for your weekend gig. Do not work on your freelance projects while you should be finishing your company's clients' request. Do not leave your job early to be on time for your gig. Do the right thing. This means carefully picking a gig that does not require you to work at times when you should be devoted to your primary employer. Maintain your integrity at your job and do your best work. It is a moral duty.

Put in the effort, be serious

I agree with Ramana Maharshi on the topic

of effort. Success only comes to those who persevere and have heart. Put as much effort into your secondary source of income as you do your job and vice versa; you will be amazed by the results. Did you know that Merriam-Webster defines *integrity* as "the quality or the state of being complete and undivided"?[2] When you are not the same person in all situations and you do not give the same intensity to your duties, you eventually lose your identity. You lose the trust and confidence of those around you. Your credibility becomes worthless. As millennials, we must keep true to ourselves and stay consistent. If we give 100% to our jobs, it makes sense to give 100% to our own ventures. Similarly, when we are giving 100% to our own ventures, we must give the same to our jobs while we still have them.

Be willing to fail but learn from your faux-pas and adjust

A survey of millennials revealed that 64% of us would rather start our own businesses than get a second job. I stand on the side of those 64%. If you are like me, you do not want to work for someone else to create more income for yourself after having worked 8 hours already for your primary employer. Great. But remember that entrepreneurship or freelancing is a path of ups and downs. Before you start on your journey of independence, you must be open to failures. You will come across road blocks, resistance and rejection. You may even experience humiliation as you are perfecting your craft and still learning. It will take more downs than ups, but the few ups will take you places you've never imagined. As renowned leadership guru John Maxwell teaches, learn from your faux-pas. Your failures are only final when you quit. Take heart and keep on. Many people think success and failure work as shown in figure 1 below. Yet, ask any successful person in any endeavor and they will tell you that success and failure work as shown in figure 2.

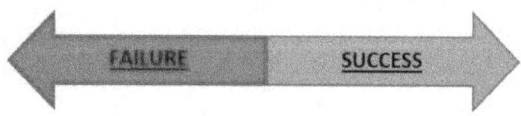

Figure 1

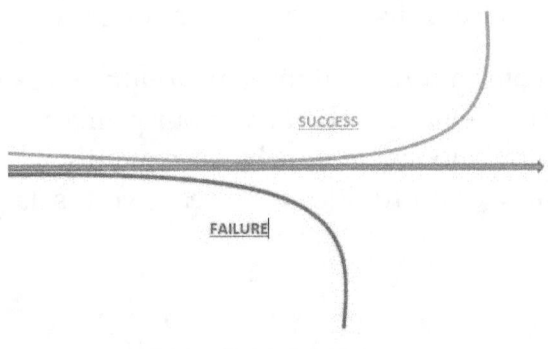

Figure 2

You will encounter failure on your path to success.

I want to share with you a few exceptional quotes on failure.

- "Only those who dare to fail greatly can ever achieve greatly." - Robert F. Kennedy

- "Success is stumbling from failure to failure with no loss of enthusiasm." - Winston Churchill

- "I have not failed. I've just found 10,000 ways that won't work." - Thomas Edison

- "My great concern is not whether you have failed, but whether you are content with your failure." - Abraham Lincoln

- "Failure is the condiment that gives success its flavor." - Truman Capote

Your failures will forge in you the work ethic and the relentless character your primary employer looks for which consequently will lead to more opportunities to increase your salary.

Develop yourself

The average American watches over five hours of television per day[3]. Unfortunately for most people, TV has become their second 'unpaid' job. Did you know that today's teens spend more than nine hours on social media every day?[4] That is more than a quarter of the day spent on social media. It is unproductive time which could be used wisely. Millennials, we have got to take advantage of these unproductive pockets of time by developing our minds and expand our knowledge on topics we value. I have come to discover that reading is the best way to enrich one's mind. I know that

An increase in your income will be relative to your leadership skills, your people skills, your winning attitude and your mindset.

reading is an unpopular practice for our generation, but we must get back to it. A few years ago, I came across *The Magic of Thinking Big* by David Schwartz and it absolutely changed my life. Then I read books such as *Think and Grow Rich* and *The Master Keys to Riches* by Napoleon Hill, *The Greatest Miracle in The World*, *Everyone Communicates, Few Connect*, *How to Win Friends and Influence People*, etc. I can guarantee you that I've made thousands of dollars and gotten several promotions at my job just from applying the mindset and the wisdom which I have acquired through reading those exceptionally written masterpieces. Reading engages your brain in ways that no amount of TV could match. I have made it a point to maintain a consistent reading schedule. Every year, I make a list of ten to twelve books to read.

You might be scratching your head now, wondering how reading is related to increasing one's income. Here is why. Joyce E. A. Russell is the Helen and William O'Toole Dean of the Villanova School of Business and licensed. She has more than 25 years of experience coaching executives and consulting on leadership and career management. In an article in the Washington Post, she asserts that "In today's highly competitive world, it is often the softer skills that differentiate applicants, and determine who will get hired, who will be successful and who will move up in the organization."[5] She goes on to say that soft skills such as integrity, work ethic, team player, positive attitude, effective communication and confidence, openness to feedback, creative thinking, problem solving and conflict management are some of the skills that differentiate one candidate from the other. It is important to develop yourself. When you are starting your own business or freelancing, you will develop a large clientele because you have acquired those soft skills as well. Your technical skills can and will only take you so far. An increase in your income will be relative to your leaderships skills, your people skills, your winning attitude and your mindset. Those skills are not taught in college textbooks. So, on the journey to becoming a money-smart millennial, we must intentionally develop ourselves. It will determine how much extra income we can generate. Moreover, once we attain a level of success our level of personal development will control our ability to maintain the income and even expand it.

Network and build connections

You've heard it many times: in a professional environment, advancement and growth are as much about who you know as what you know and sometimes who you know is even more important than what you know. I have experienced it first-hand myself. The more people know your name from a positive encounter they've had with you - you will create more positive relations by developing your people skills as mentioned in the previous section - the more they are willing to vouch for you and give you opportunities to grow. But let me be clear here. This is not about being nice to everyone and letting people walk all over you. Networking and building connections requires you to become a positive asset which others count on. Offer to be a helping hand when others need it, go the extra mile when a task is expected of you, build bridges among your coworkers or clients and always aim at producing competent and quality work. Thus, your connections will reciprocate your attitude towards them.

Offer to be a helping hand when others need it, go the extra mile when a task is expected of you, build bridges among your coworkers or clients and always aim at producing competent and quality work.

On your journey to moving up in your career or developing a secondary income to meet financial stability, there will be instances when you will need a helping hand. If you have not built useful relationships and connections, it will be too late to develop them and you will lose on major opportunities. Professional networking is a must in today's world. Most job recruiters will tell you that it is much more effective to use referrals to land a job than to simply apply online on career sites. Websites such as www.meetup.com or www.eventbrite.com offer so many opportunities to meet other professionals in your industry. With Meetup, you can attend events where other individuals share your interests. In those instances, a connection foundation is laid for you and all you have to do is to introduce yourself. As millennials, we should seize those opportunities. Are you a business owner or an entrepreneur? If your answer to that question is yes, I highly recommend that you purchase and read *The Referral of a Lifetime* by Tim Templeton. It is undeniably one of the best books I've read on developing a successful network. A few years ago, I was a shy 20-year-old millennial who could barely start a conversation. But I was envious of the individuals who always had a bubbly personality and who could meet anyone, anywhere. I still remember going to Barnes & Noble and buying *How to talk to anyone* by Leil

Lowndes. Since then, I have been recommended and have read tons of other books on social skills: *How to Win Friends and Influence People, Bringing Out the Best In People, The Friendship Factor, How To Start A Conversation and Make Friends, Wired That Way* and many more. These books have taught me skills which I have used to develop a considerable network today. It's your turn to start. Take the initiative. I am still today a bit of an introvert but I've learned and studied the skills necessary to create and foster productive friendships and professional relationships.

Master your craft

Growing up and going through middle school and high school, I constantly heard my father say: 'Whatever you do, become the best at it'. In our household, there wasn't a question of whether we were good in mathematics but bad in composition, good in English but bad in history. If we

Mastering your craft will be the difference between getting paid very well and getting paid to barely make the time investment worth it.

were graded on it, we were encouraged to get the best grade possible. So, when I got home after learning about a new notion in math or physics, I would do every single exercise and problem available related to the subject. The goal was to become familiar with every nuance of the topic that could possibly be presented to me on an exam. The result: I was an A student virtually in every subject. By the way, I never felt pressured by my parents. Au contraire, I was consistently encouraged and told that I had potential that I had not tapped into, and they believed in me.

To this day, I believe that I was not more intelligent than everybody else. Yes, I may have had some talent in some subjects, but I practiced so many times that I knew how to handle any problem. Any athlete who has attained a level of success will tell you that they have applied the same principle in their life. Practice, practice and more practice. Repetition ameliorates your skill level and it also reveals your weaknesses. Then knowing what you could improve on gives you the chance to become even better at your craft. My point is that once you have chosen what to do to increase your income, study it and strive to be very good, if not an expert at it. In return, mastering your craft will be the difference between getting paid very well and getting paid to barely make the time investment worth it.

In the next chapter, I will give you a few

examples and ideas on how to expand your income.

Chapter II: Ways to increase your cash flow

Educationists should build the capacities of the spirit of inquiry, creativity, entrepreneurial and moral leadership among students and become their role model. - A. P. J. Abdul Kalam

Now that you've decided that you want to increase your income, it is time to choose how. The criteria were laid out in the previous chapter and they should serve as a guide. This chapter is meant to give you ideas and examples. They are not the only options. Be creative, think big, think for yourself, be money-smart.

Try entrepreneurship and launch your own business

There are many ways to increase one's income. However, they are not all created equal. I believe business ownership is the most stable and long term path to venture on when looking to expand income for financial stability. Starting small gigs or getting part time jobs are temporary solutions and they do have their value. Secondary jobs have the potential of generating the necessary income a household may need to get its finances back on track. Nonetheless, they do not compare in results to the production of an established enterprise of your own. In the twenty-first century, business ownership does not have to equate to a building, an office, some heavy-duty machinery or multiple employees. Therefore, entrepreneurship is accessible to more of us millennials than less.

One day at work, I received a call from a client whom I had been trying to get in touch with for months. She finally called me back eight months after my first attempt at getting her to meet me and wanted to know why I had been meaning to introduce myself. Well, as any other good banker would do, I had to bring enough value right then and there to convince her to meet me. Mrs. S. is a business owner who had close to $90,000 in her personal checking account which was an individual account. My first thought was to add a beneficiary. Mrs. S. couldn't wait another day. She was sitting in my office the next. While getting to know my client, I learned that her daughter Beth who is a millennial is a successful business owner as well. What does she do? She is a real estate stager. A few years prior, Beth was exposed to real estate staging, realized that she had a talent, saw an opportunity and took a leap of faith. Just three years later, Beth was running her own business and was doing very well at it.

Ahmed, another client of mine couldn't keep a job to save his life. A hard worker but an entrepreneur at heart, Ahmed also took a leap of faith and started his mobile auto detailing business. He borrowed money from his parents and the bank and bought a van and some equipment. Here we are just a couple years later and he's about to purchase another van.

The path of entrepreneurship is not an easy one. In fact, it is probably ten times harder than the road travelled by employees. However, when I interview entrepreneurs, they always praise how rewarding the work is. Rarely do I see a business owner who would rather be an employee. On the other side, one in two millennials want to start a business or already has one established. 35% of millennials who have a job have also started their own business[1]. I believe the millennial years are the best years to venture into business ownership. For most of us millennials, the risk is minimal. Let me explain. The older you get, the more responsibilities you have. These may include a family to support, a mortgage to pay, an established career, etc. People who dream of

> *In the twenty-first century, business ownership does not have to equate to a building, an office, some heavy-duty machinery or multiple employees.*

being their own bosses give up on their dreams crippled by the fear of failing and putting their families at risk. We've all heard that 50% of small business fail within the first 5 years of existence. Yes, it is a scary thought, but it's even scarier for an entrepreneur who has a family to feed. In the case of millennials, we are just starting our careers, many of us are yet to be married and do not have a family to care for. So, go for it. Take that ten-thousand-pound step. It may be the beginning of an incredibly exciting and rewarding life.

The case for direct sales businesses

It's six o'clock in the evening, you left the office a few minutes ago and there is your cell phone ringing. It's your friend Zach who is calling. After catching up a bit, five minutes later Zach is telling you about a new business he's started with a company in direct sales. He's excited and is also offering you the opportunity to work with him. Have you received such a call? If you haven't, I can guarantee you that it will happen sooner or later. Before you decline Zach's offer and rebuke him, I suggest taking time to examine what he is offering and consider the legitimacy of the business. Direct sales companies have long been tagged 'pyramid schemes'. Before we go any further, let me clarify that 'pyramid schemes' are illegal. Unless these companies have somehow managed to hide billions of dollars in transactions from the Internal Revenue Service, the Federal Trade Commission and the federal government for decades, we are in big trouble because our authorities have outrageously failed. In 2016, there were more than twenty million people involved in direct sales and the industry generated more than thirty-six billion dollars[2]. There are substantial and lucrative opportunities in direct sales.

I mentioned earlier that I believe that entrepreneurship is the most stable path to financial stability. To be realistic, starting a business or becoming an entrepreneur is not as easy as it sounds. For the majority of 'entrepreneurs at heart', the first step into entrepreneurship is never taken or it is delayed due to these obstacles: risk, expertise, capital to invest and time. Most multi-level (direct sales) businesses do not involve those obstacles. Are there risks involved in starting a business with a direct selling or multi-level marketing company? Like any other venture, there are. But these risks are minimal in comparison with traditional business ownership as the investment is usually just a couple hundred dollars. One can continue working a full-time job while building their business on a part-time basis, a fact that resolves the issue with time. In chapter I, I told you to choose an opportunity that will not interfere with your current job. A direct selling business allows to do so. Many multi-level marketing companies offer extensive training, coaching and support and a platform allowing individuals to run their businesses without handling logistics. A few years ago, I was introduced to the industry and I have had an exceptional experience. In fact, I attribute the success that I've had in other areas of my private and professional lives to the leadership skills that I've learned working with a multi-level company. Working our business as a couple, Heather and I have something in common that we get to do after we have clocked out for our respective jobs. We share successes and challenges. We strategize together and encourage each other. I am aware that there are thousands of blogs on the web that will warn you about venturing into the direct selling world. Occasionally, I come across the terrifying story of an individual who was involved in a multi-level business and had a terrible experience. Through the years, I've come to realize that such experiences are usually the results of the malpractice of certain independent business owners. Their lack of integrity, morals, honesty and leadership leads to the deterioration of the industry's image and particularly of the companies they represent.

Per the direct selling association, women still constitute the majority of direct sellers in the USA but as the industry is changing with a diversity of products and services offered, men are quickly joining the game as well. In 2015, the industry sold more than $12 billion worth of wellness products, more than $7 billion in services and a combined $12 plus billions in home and personal care items. These may not be the fanciest products but the Walton family did not become one of the richest families in the country by selling the latest technology items.

In his book *The Business of the 21st Century*, successful businessman and author Robert Kiyosaki clears the fog on the concept of network marketing. I strongly recommend reading the book if you are a millennial. Not all companies are made equal. There are hundreds of multilevel marketing companies out there and if you are going to partner with one, here are some of the key points to consider:

- A proven system of support, training and coaching should be established to guide you.

- The products offered should be of high quality with a reasonable guarantee policy and most importantly, I believe they should be consumables (or services) which the public uses on a regular basis.

- Marketing of the company's products should be doable without extensive technical training. This trait goes along with the marketability of products to the public.

- Compensation should be exclusively based on revenue generated, not on numbers of recruits.

- The purchase of training and support material should be optional and at the business owner's discretion.

Fellow millennials, there was a time when a long career guaranteed a pension and Social Security benefits which provided a decent life during the retirement years. Well, since 2010, the Social Security Administration's cash flow has been in the red as more benefits are being paid than taxes collected[3]. It is almost a certainty that our future benefits will be reduced unless dramatic changes are executed by Congress. In my line of work, I see what the benefits are for most people and trust me, it is nothing to brag about. Scaling back on those already modest Social Security benefit payments will make them insignificant down the road. Developing an additional income using a direct sales business model might just be the lifesaver.

Gigs

Compared to part time jobs, freelance gigs usually pay more. They are also temporary, but when done well the return on your time will most likely be higher. A gig may be your doorway into business ownership.

Become a tutor

You've spent thousands of dollars to acquire your degree, so put it to great use. Those six months that you spent abroad in Spain learning Spanish should now pay you dollars. Maximize the return on your (parents') investment in your education. Heck, you may not be a wizard in mathematics, but are you comfortable with elementary math and pre-algebra? How about study skills, composition, English or even a sport such as tennis? There are many websites which would link you to students in need of help in diverse subjects. My favorite is wyzant.com. Though their service fee is quite high for your very first hours, it is possible to make a substantial income from the website. As I mentioned earlier, Heather and I took advantage of our skills in French and math and made a lot cash. We also capitalized on craigslist.com where we did not have to pay any percentage of our revenues back. In the Washington DC area, tutoring a handful of kids a couple times a week, at a rate of $40 - $50 per hour can go very far in terms of additional income. When tutoring, it is important to be truthful in terms of your competencies. I remember going to a tutee's home the first time and being faced with a problem in statistics. Even while I was in high school and college, statistics was not my strong suit and after years of virtually no practice, I was clueless. I immediately let the high schooler and her parents know that I could not help her. I apologized and committed to find another tutor for her. I also told them that they did not have to pay me. They appreciated my transparency; they still paid me and even left a good review on my profile.

Capitalize on your programming skills and other talents

In today's world of technology, programming is a skill that is very sought after. Per the Bureau of Labor Statistics, hourly rates for computer programmers as employees can be as high as $62.89 on average[4]. Independently, programmers can charge even more for their services. If you are a programmer, though you are in a very competitive industry, there are still many opportunities for freelance work. So, offer your skills to build websites, create and design apps, design logos, etc. Create a profile on websites such as fiverr.com and be on your way to a taste of entrepreneurship. However, keep in mind that for such an opportunity, there will be a 'ramp-up' season to meet a level of permanent and profitable work. Do not expect it to be easy. Persistence will be the key to your success as president Calvin Coolidge so eloquently said: 'Nothing in this world can take the place of persistence. Talent will not: nothing is more common than unsuccessful men with talent. Genius will not; unrewarded genius is almost a proverb. Education will not: the world is full of educated derelicts. Persistence and determination alone are omnipotent.'

> *Nothing in this world can take the place of persistence. Talent will not: nothing is more common than unsuccessful men with talent. Genius will not; unrewarded genius is almost a proverb. Education will not: the world is full of educated derelicts. Persistence and determination alone are omnipotent.*

Rent your space

Ilias and Sonia, clients of mine, recently bought their first home in the heart of the very expensive Montgomery County, MD. They both love travelling, especially back to Ukraine where Ilias is from. On average, each trip costs them about $2500 and although they both make decent incomes as engineers, they wanted to save that sum of money instead. Sonia came across www.airbnb.com while on Facebook and together, they decided to give it a try. With two available bedrooms and no pets, their home attracted many visitors. Just a few months later, Ilias and Sonia told me about how they had made enough to cover the next trip and how by the end of that year, their monthly revenues would easily pay their mortgage dues.

If you are comfortable having strangers as guests in your home on a regular basis, generating income by renting your available space might be the solution for you. For safety, Airbnb offers peace of mind through a '$1,000,000 host guarantee' and host protection insurance. Similar websites include FlipKey, HomeAway and OneFineStay.

Drive for a rideshare company

Do you live in or are you close to cities

including New York City, San Francisco, Boston or Washington DC? If so, driving for Uber might be worth the time and effort. According to a Time magazine article, drivers in those cities make an average of $19 per hour after their own investment. In New York City, the hourly rate averages $30.35[5].

I'm not particularly a fan of this option but if you choose to go that route, I recommend doing enough research to make your investment worthwhile. It is definitely a temporary solution to creating additional income. The important thing for any millennial is to act and do something. I've met millennials who would not get any job or do any gig because it is 'below' their education or degrees.

> *One cannot feed his ego and his family at the same time.*

They live with mom and dad, are broke and bored and are just waiting for the 'right job' to magically show up in their lap. Life does not work that way, friends. I learned this lesson a long time ago and have kept it: *one cannot feed his ego and his family at the same time*. Sometimes you must do what's necessary for yourself and for your family even when your ego is affected. That's what makes your victory over your struggle even more powerful. The movie *Cinderella Man* illustrates it so beautifully.

Personal training

Obtaining a personal trainer license may also be a profitable investment. Rachel, a 25-year-old nurse and part time personal trainer was able to acquire a handful of clients. She met with them for training sessions on a weekly basis. Her rate was not extravagant. Nonetheless at $30 per hour, meeting once or twice a week with each client whom by the way was a friend or a family member, Rachel made over $1000 per month before tax.

Are you into fitness and exercising? Do you enjoy coaching and giving instructions? Are you one to maintain a healthy lifestyle and diet? Do you like being independent and making your own decisions? If you answered 'yes' to one or all these questions, personal training might be for you.

Amateur 'paid' photography

For fun, perform a Google search of 'photographers near me'. Once you have a list of four or five photography businesses, look up their rates and you will see how expensive photography services can be. In the Washington, D.C. area, an engagement session can easily cost upward of $500 or more. I did that search on

Google and found a local photographer who charges $250 per hour for family portraits and $150 for individual portraits. On another photographer's website, the pricing page shows that wedding rates start at $3100. In your state or region of the country, photography services may not be as high-priced, but what I'm conveying is that there is profit to be made. Does that mean that anybody should buy a camera and start a photography business? Absolutely not.

First, buying DSLR cameras are a huge financial investment. Whether you purchase a new one or a used one on eBay, it will cost you a few hundred dollars. Second, simply owning such a device does not make you a photographer worthy of getting paid for services. It takes talent and a certain creative and artistic eye that many do not have. The job of a photographer is to capture stories of people and places in a way that stirs emotions and brings back memories. If you cannot do that, then photography is not for you.

Throughout the book, you see a random picture at the beginning of parts I, II and III. They are photographs that I have taken. Growing up, I was a very creative and artistic kid. I could look at a drawing and reproduce it easily. When I bought my Nikon D3200 three years ago, I discovered that I had another talent: photography. It's become a 'paid hobby' for me. Some of my photographs are posted on my

Instagram account and on Facebook. Through exposure, I have gotten the opportunity to photograph some of my connections and friends who paid me for the service.

In conclusion, if you believe you have a talent in photography, go for it. You do not have to be established as a business. You may need to build your portfolio by offering free sessions at first. Reach out to friends and family, offer your services at a lower price than the competition, and you will soon be making a few hundred extra dollars to supplement your income.

Part-time jobs

I would recommend obtaining a part time job as my last resort. In my opinion, part time jobs generally do not produce enough to be worth the time invested. However, for some millennials, it may be the only alternative. So, my recommendation for you is to find one that pays well.

Ashley was in dire need of additional income. In college, she had worked at a bar as a server and made enough to help pay for her tuition. She contacted the owner who graciously offered her to work again a few nights per week. Working Wednesdays, Fridays and some Saturdays, she made enough with her tips to cover her car note and insurance payments.

I once met a gentleman while waiting for my car to be serviced at a shop in Frederick, MD. He was the office manager/front desk clerk and since I was the only one in the lobby, we couldn't help but talk to each other. The conversation led to the topic of part time jobs. Here was his story. For a period of five to seven years, he had worked as a pizza delivery employee for a local restaurant. His weekly income averaged about $500 and he saved every bit of it. With discipline, he stored it away at the bank and never touched the funds. His claim to fame: he bought his first home with one lump-sum from the savings he had accumulated from his pizza delivery job over the period of half a dozen years.

Other opportunities to generate extra income

Handyman? Offer your contracting skills.
Babysit.
Many more. Be creative.

The End

Dear millennial, we are at the end of *Money-Smart Millennials*. As a recap, here is what you've learned.

In Part 1, we established ow to set up a personal budget and how to live your life in accordance with your budget plan.

Then in Part 2, you acquired tips about banking, debt and credit and you were also given a winning mindset to make money-smart choices.

Finally, Part 3 taught you the state of mind required to expand your income. In addition, you learned about a few ways to develop a supplemental income. You are now equipped with a mindset that will propel you on your journey to financial stability.

As I said at the beginning of the book, financial stability is a stepping stone. It is a foundation to build upon. Nothing can be built on a soft foundation.

I've enjoyed this journey with you and I hope you have too. This is just the beginning. If you struggle financially today, I hope you will take your finances back with the skills you've learned in this book. I hope you will not postpone for another day, another month, another year. Nobody gets time back; once it's gone it is lost. It is our most precious commodity. In just a few years, you may become a father, a mother, a homeowner. Someone may depend on you to survive. Are you going be a failure financially? Are you going to be the one making excuses? You do not have to because now you know how to start outsmarting money. You can be in control. Start today. Do not delay your success and financial stability. I see a bright future for millennials. Our world is full of opportunities to seize. Be a Money-Smart Millennial.

Success is a team effort. So, I am inviting you to join my team so we can work together toward your goal. The next step is to subscribe to my articles on moneysmartmillenials.com and send me your thoughts about the money-smart mindset and your money goals at lionel@moneysmartmillennials.com.

Finally, if you enjoyed this book and learned from it, then I'd like to ask you a favor. Would you be kind enough to leave a review on Amazon? I'd appreciate your insight.

Thank you and let's start this incredible journey to becoming a money-smart millennial!

Notes

Introduction

1. "Millennials Outnumber Baby Boomers and Are Far More Diverse." Millennials Outnumber Baby Boomers and Are Far More Diverse. N.p., 25 June 2015. Web. 3 Mar. 2016.
http://www.census.gov/newsroom/press-releases/2015/cb15-113.html
2. Edelman, Ric. "Why So Many Lottery Winners Go Broke." Fortune Why So Many Lottery Winners Go Broke Comments. N.p., 14 Jan. 2016. Web. 2 Feb. 2016.
http://fortune.com/2016/01/15/powerball-lottery-winners/

Part I

Chapter I:

1. Allison, Kent E. "Financial Stress Surging Among Millennials." The Huffington Post. TheHuffingtonPost.com, 27 Apr. 2016. Web. May-June 2016.
http://www.huffingtonpost.com/kent-e-allison/financial-stress-surging-among-millennials_b_9787658.html
2. Feeney, Nolan. "Millennials Now Largest Generation in the U.S. Labor Force." Time. Time, 11 May 2015. Web. 02 Apr. 2016.

http://time.com/3854518/millennials-labor-force/

3. Fromm, Jeff. "Millennials In The Workplace: They Don't Need Trophies But They Want Reinforcement." Forbes. Forbes Magazine, 6 Nov. 2015. Web. 02 Apr. 2016. http://www.forbes.com/sites/jefffromm/2015/11/06/millennials-in-the-workplace-they-dont-need-trophies-but-they-want-reinforcement/2/#68229f061eb6

4. "Millennials Infographic." Goldman Sachs. N.p., 2016. Web. 07 June 2016. http://www.goldmansachs.com/our-thinking/pages/millennials/

5. Farrington, Robert. "Failure To Follow Up: The Sad Truth About Millennial Financial Literacy." Forbes. Forbes Magazine, 8 Jan. 2015. Web. 7 June 2016. http://www.forbes.com/sites/robertfarrington/2015/01/08/failure-to-follow-up-the-sad-truth-about-millennial-financial-literacy/#13232f4127f2

6. Imbert, Fred. "Millennials Make Unrealistic Retirement Plans." CNBC. CNBC, 28 Sept. 2015. Web. 8 Apr. 2016. http://www.cnbc.com/2015/09/28/study-millennials-make-unrealistic-retirement-plans.html

7. "FINRA Foundation Study Finds Millennials Struggle Financially."

Www.finra.org. N.p., n.d. Web. 07 May
2016.
**https://www.finra.org/newsroom/2014/fi
nra-foundation-study-finds-millennials-
struggle-financially**

Chapter III:

1. Mendes, Elizabeth. "Americans Spend
    $151 a Week on Food; the High-Income,
    $180." Gallup.com. N.p., 02 Aug. 2012.
    Web. 16 May 2016.
    **http://www.gallup.com/poll/156416/amer
    icans-spend-151-week-food-high-
    income-180.aspx**
2. Elkins, Kathleen. "Here's How Much
    Money Millennials Are Earning in Each
    State." Business Insider. Business Insider,
    Inc, 07 Apr. 2015. Web. 03 June 2016.
    **http://www.businessinsider.com/the-
    average-salary-of-millennials-2015-3**
3. "Credit Union vs. Bank - Benefits &
    Which Is Better." Credit Union vs. Bank -
    Benefits & Which Is Better. N.p., n.d.
    Web. 3 June 2016.
    **http://www.bankrate.com/finance/credit-
    unions/pros-cons-credit-unions-5.aspx**

Part II

Chapter I:

1. "Delayed Gratification: Definition and Overview." Study.com. N.p., n.d. Web. 13 Mar. 2016.
http://study.com/academy/lesson/delaye d-gratification-definition-lesson-quiz.html

2. "Credit Union vs. Bank - Benefits & Which Is Better." Credit Union vs. Bank - Benefits & Which Is Better. N.p., n.d. Web. 25 June 2016.
http://www.bankrate.com/finance/credit-unions/pros-cons-credit-unions-5.aspx

Chapter II:

1. "Don't buy your laptop twice. when accidents strike, we've got you covered." Laptop Insurance. N.p., n.d. Web. 26 Mar. 2016.
https://www.squaretrade.com/laptop-warranty

Part III

Chapter I:

1. Walsh, Ben. "Sorry, But Saving Money Won't Make You Rich." The Huffington Post. TheHuffingtonPost.com, 03 Nov. 2014. Web. 28 Sept. 2016.

http://www.huffingtonpost.com/2014/11/
03/saving-wont-make-you-
rich_n_6094802.html

2. Merriam-Webster. Merriam-Webster, n.d.
Web. 02 Aug. 2016. http://www.merriam-
webster.com/dictionary/integrity

3. Koblin, John. "How Much Do We Love
TV? Let Us Count the Ways." The New
York Times. The New York Times, 03
June 2016. Web. 17 Sept. 2016.
http://www.nytimes.com/2016/07/01/busi
ness/media/nielsen-survey-media-
viewing.html

4. Wallace, Kelly. "Teens Spend 9 Hours a
Day Using Media, Report Says." CNN.
Cable News Network, 3 Nov. 2015. Web.
15 Apr. 2016.
http://www.cnn.com/2015/11/03/health/te
ens-tweens-media-screen-use-
report/index.html

5. Russell, Joyce E. A, PhD. Washington
Post. The Washington Post, 16 Mar. 2014.
Web. 3 Sept. 2016.
https://www.washingtonpost.com/busin
ess/capitalbusiness/2014/03/14/ccd6725c-
aa21-11e3-9e82-8064fcd31b5b_story.html

Chapter II:

1. Tredgold, Gordon. "29 Surprising Facts
That Explain Why Millennials See the

World Differently." Inc.com. N.p., 02 May
2016. Web. 05 July 2016.
http://www.inc.com/gordon-tredgold/29-surprising-facts-about-millennials-and-what-motivates-them.html

2. "Industry Fact Sheets." Industry Fact
   Sheets. Direct Selling Association, n.d.
   Web. 17 June 2016.
   http://www.dsa.org/benefits/research/factsheets

3. "Will Social Security Still Exist When I
   Retire?" CNNMoney. Cable News
   Network, n.d. Web. 06 June 2016.
   http://money.cnn.com/retirement/guide/SocialSecurity_basics.moneymag/index18.htm

4. "15-1131 Computer Programmers." U.S.
   Bureau of Labor Statistics. U.S. Bureau of
   Labor Statistics, May 2015. Web. 28 Apr.
   2016.
   http://www.bls.gov/oes/current/oes151131.htm

5. Davidson, Jacob. "Uber Reveals How
   Much Its Drivers Really Earn...Sort Of."
   Time. Time, 22 Jan. 2015. Web. 08 May
   2016.
   http://time.com/money/3678389/uber-drivers-wages/

www.moneysmartmillennials.com

lionel@moneysmartmillennials.com